CHASERS OF THE SUN:
CREEK INDIAN THOUGHTS

CHASERS OF THE SUN:
CREEK INDIAN THOUGHTS

By Louis Littlecoon Oliver

The Greenfield Review Press
Greenfield Center, New York

All rights reserved. No part of this book may be used or reproduced in any manner whatsoever without written permission except in the case of brief quotations embodied in critical articles and reviews.

Thanks to the following publications where some of these poems first appeared: *Northeast Indian Quarterly, Mildred, The Wooster Review.*

Publication of the book has been made possible in part through Literary publishing grants from the National Endowment for the Arts Literature Program and the New York State Council on the Arts.

ISBN 0-912678-70-4

Copyright © 1990 Louis Oliver

LC# 87-80182

FIRST EDITION

Composition by Sans Serif, Ann Arbor, MI 48104
Printed in the United States of America

Cover art by Louis Littlecoon Oliver

Contents

PART ONE:

Chasers of the Sun

Chasers of the Sun

The only explanation of the origin of the Muskoke (Creek) tribe with veracity, was told by an ancient one by the name of Chikili. Because the ethnologists pressured him for a revelation he told the following with a twinkle in his eye: "We came pouring out of the backbone of this continent like ants. We saw for the first time a great ball of fire rising out of the earth in the east. We were astounded at the phenomena, but we had no fear of it. We held council and made a decision to go and find the place that it lived. All the world was new to us and before us lay a great plain with much grass. We discussed how we should travel in a straight line and one of the prophets said: "Let the seed arrow show us the way, we will shoot it as far as we can and if we find it standing straight up, we will continue to do this until we find the home of the ball of fire."

On our journey eastward we saw great herds of animals— so many that in their roaming they shook the earth and hid themselves in clouds of dust. We would shoot the arrow again and follow it until the ball of fire disappeared and we camped. Our spirit fed and nourished us. Our old ones often spoke their wisdom that gave us strength and hope for our quest. Again and again we followed the arrow until at one time we found it laying with its point towards us. We were at the banks of a wide and muddy river, so we pitched camp. Through the dark hours the prophet pondered our next move. His decision was to study the river and determine how to cross it, or whether to live here until the "Spirit" moved us. In his meditations it came to him that the ball of fire was still much farther away, but that a way would be made to continue their search of its abode. Here they built temporary huts covered with mud and grass. They were supplied with fish as food. Scouts were sent up rivers to find the possibility of crossing. For the first time they met another tribe, who used boats, but were not friendly and spoke a language they did not understand. They came back and made the report of their finding. "Fear not" the prophet said, "our spirit will move

3

them to gentleness and we will use their method of crossing rivers."

"So it was" Chikili said and they found themselves in a new country, a paradise with forests, clear cold streams and mountains. For a stretch of time they settled on a clear river, by which they found an ancient stone marker with marks scratched which they did not understand, but called it "Chatohochee," which interpreted meant "a rock with writings."

For a time, perhaps for years, they settled here, built log huts or used caves to live in. There was still that desire to further chase the sun to its home, so upon orders of the council they shot the red arrow eastward and followed it again. They came in contact with other inhabitants who were Indian, but bypassed them. They noticed that the forests and clean waters were vast and extensive. They came to a long range of mountains similar to one they came out of. There they camped for a time. They shot the arrow again and again for many moons and finally it stood on the beach of the great white waters. They camped, for the darkness had come and weariness overcame them.

Confounded, the prophet never slept, so he was first to see the sun rise up out of the great white waters. He aroused the others to see and they stood in wonderment – nonplussed. The prophet said: "Now we know that the great ball of fire lives in those waters, and also we do not understand how that can be. We can only turn back and find a permanent place to live." So they did, Chikili said, and settled on a river they called Okmologee.

These people, this tribe I have mentioned did actually settle on the river mentioned (Okmulgee). They were not organized, and were like "babes in the woods." In time there appeared four men among them, one saying: "I am Yahola and we are sent from the high sky by the Creator of the great ball of fire which you will call in your language, Ha'se." They mingled with the Creeks as if they were one of them. Yahola continued: "We will show you and teach you how to live and the way you should live."

4

So it did happen and at the end of their full instructions, they, the visiting spirits, were lifted up and disappeared into the sky. One of their prophecies happened in this manner; There came such a darkness over the earth that the fowl of the air, the wild animals and denizens of the deep could not see, for a period of thirty days. In that obsidian darkness they wandered about by feel and instinct.

Various species of the animal kingdom came into the homes of the Creeks for protection and food. The bear, the deer, the panther, the snake and birds. By the sanction and purpose of the Great Spirit the Indians accepted them and claimed relationship with them as a clan. Though at one time there were a dozen or more clans there are only seven today, namely: Bear, Deer, Bird, Wind, Potato, Racoon and Panther (Tigers). This happened due to the dying out of the ancient ones. So according to the instructions of the four angels a Chief and his assistant built their square or in our language the Bighouse (Chukorako). Its foundation, spiritually, were four logs cut the same length and laid in the direction of the four cardinal points, east, west, north and south. In the center, space is left for the fire which as yet they had not performed the method of creating it. With all things, the Creeks were told, there must be a ceremony or ritual as we taught you. One man had been pointed out as the Master of Fire. He and his assistants found the tinder (tokpvfka) in Sycamore wood. On a block of dried and seasoned Elm, a dried and hard stem of Cane (Kohv) was used to drill on it and cause spontaneous combustion onto the tinder. No other method was to be used to obtain fire as it was a holy thing and considered a gift of the Great Spirit. The fire was not to be started until the plan and layout of the bighouse was completed. One each side of the fire a brush arbor was built. The one on the west was considered the Chief's bed which was partitioned off for the notables such as the vice chief (e'mapoktv) the medicine man (Hilishvya) the precious person (hemeha) and the judge (Fvcechv) The seats were primitive with logs across blocks. The Chief's bed was elevated, covered with bark and Cane. In the first section north were seated the Wind and Bear clan, and in the south the medicine man (hilishaya) the hemeha who was of the Bird clan and the Beaver clan. The Chief was of the Bird clan. In the north arbor were the messengers called Big Emathla and Little Emathla. On the east was the Warrior's bed called Tustenuke. The south arbor was for the rest of the clans and visitors called este coloke. At the northeast corner of the Chief's bed were placed two pots of medicine. A little north of the emathla arbor was the house of precious articles. The women entered the grounds from the southwest. The ball ground was usually a little northeast of the square. Outside of the square were brush arbors for families and their children.

Now it is in the month of the Big harvest moon (hayothlakko) or August, and the green corn is at its best. As per the wish of Yahola it is the Creeks' new year and they will have their first celebration or "Busk" as it is referred to by the Anglo-Americans. The square is ready for the fire to be built – the tribe is ready for the fast. I hope the world can better understand why the Indian is so different in pathos and intellect than the Anglos, as I present them in my less scholarly way.

The master of the fire feeds it to the wood brought up by his assistants, then he marks a circle around it about twenty-five feet in diameter, which makes the area sacred and holy. No one is to enter it except the master, the medicine man and the person who supplies wood to the fire. If a child or a person unknowingly trespasses the limits, the spirit and the holiness of the fire is desecrated, so that a new one has to be built. Being true to their belief, it has never happened.

I add here a note to further bolster our beliefs: Contemporary man although rejecting fantasy and myth, aspires to make it a reality. True for man to fly was a fantasy, but he does just that now, but only mechanically. What he cannot grasp is the irrelevance of Spirit to matter. Spirit, as the term is used, is in the sense of a broad generalization. The gods, and there are many gods, rule in this outer world, each delegated with a power peculiar to its governing law. This is one

6

group of beings (spirits) as opposed to the theocratic governing body which is the fountain head of pristine laws. These spiritual entities are the *true* governors of mankind through the ages. Superstition, in the light of modern science and religion is a fantasy, but we try to become superhuman. Modern man in his attempt to super-intelligence shackles himself in matter and has not the faith to shed it, therefore, he still flounders in ignorance. Other civilizations found the key to separating matter from the ethereal or Spirit.

The fast begins in this manner; no food or water is taken in. The medicine man sends four men out to find and bring to him the roots of (Mekohoyemecv) or redroot, its properties are highly emetic. Along with that, some spicewood (kapapaska). These are made into tea in separate pots. The medicine man (Hilishaya) sings a prayer and blows it into the concoction through a hollow reed. He does this four times. At around 10 o'clock the men come with containers (gourds) to drink the warm tea of the redroot. (which by the way, its botanical name is Ilex Vomitoria). Each person knows just how much to take in before the urge to vomit happens. For some it takes alot, for others very little. Those who cannot by redroot alone go to the spicewood tea to help induce vomiting.

The reason for emptying the stomach in this manner is, they were told by the spirit Yahola, in time the lining becomes caked and interferes with its proper functioning. A healthy stomach means a healthy body. The women were not required to participate in this ritual, but allowed to administer to themselves and their children as they wished. The medicine man knew the requirements of women for medicine, and the taking of the redroot by the men was looked upon as a war physic.

At around noon or awhile afterwards, the men challenge the women to a stickball game. Usually the temperature was around 110°, but they were urged to play hard until nearly sundown. The women used their hands and the men the clubs—making it rather difficult for them to score. The

7

women always won, but the true purpose of the affair was to induce perspiration to the extent that the medicine properly circulated in the blood being purified and the waste, if any, came out through the pores of the skin.

Now I must say here that the physical stature of the Creek Indians in those days, both men and women, was superb. No man was under six foot and no woman was "baggy" or paunchy. They were all the very picture of health, as they bantered and fought for the ball, but all in good humour.

As near sundown the men single-filed to the river to bathe, a portion of which was "doctored" by the medicine man. The women went to their designated area. After the bath the men in single-file came towards the pole (Pok'vpe) singing the song taught them by Yahola. It was the end of the fast and tables of their kind of food were set. The "piece-de-resistance" was roasted corn or boiled roasting ears.

The hunters had brought in bear and deer—flayed and quartered by the women the day before; so that roasted meats were plentiful. At this time of the year wild grapes or possum grapes were fully ripe so there were pots of dumplings made of them. Their main drink was hominy, but prepared the Indian way which we call O'sofke. They pounded parched corn and sifted it to a flour consistency which they mixed with water and honey and drank it. They had food, rather exotic, too numerous to mention here. After the meal, there was a sense of euphoria and the men smoked a mixture of wild tobacco and sumac leaves.

Around 9 or 10 o'clock the so called "stomp dance" was to begin. How did they know which songs to sing? Yahola instructed them very well. I will be quoting others of like genre so as to bolster our beliefs as I have said. It has been said by the Anglos that the Indians in their songs and dances are a bunch of wild, yelling and hooping pagans, but concerning our kind of music, I quote Allen P. Merriam: "The single and most important fact about music and its relationship to the total world is its origin in the supernatural sphere." And

8

from Brian Swann: "The wilderness people were one with the unconsious and with the wilderness, there was no psychic distance between individual and song; or the reality that song expressed." And I say that the Indians were divinely inspired through Yahola, an angel of the Great Spirit, to sing and dance as they do. They have been doing this for many hundreds of years and not one iota of the songs have been changed.

So, in this instance, a leader is found and the dance starts. He walks slowly around the fire counter-clockwise, four times. The women with turtle shells strapped around their legs fall in line behind the leaders. There is a man carrying a stickball racket and acting like a deacon of a church, urging others to join in.

After his fourth round the leaders sounds out a long drawn out "yodel" so to speak, and those who have joined him, answer with a sharp "hoop." As the leader continues the man with the ball club shouts out: "Locha! Locha! Locha!" urging the shellshakers to join in. As the whole begins to "warm-up" so to speak, he again pleads "Tokas Che! hayomofa! hayomofa! Emvmiycvlke! emvmiycvlke!" (Now – Attention, attention, helpers, helpers, come on!)

To describe the action and the sound is very difficult as it involves entering into the sphere of the supernatural. Gradually the leader invokes, by stronger verses, the spirits of the other world and as the dance progresses they are all lifted up seemingly in a cloud. Many other leaders will come forward to continue the euphoria until daybreak.

The strangeness of it all is, the whole square had been "doctored" to forestall sleepiness, weariness until the sun is fully up. And then it all seems to come at once as they all prepare to leave the grounds to their respective dwellings.

This is called the break, Netvkvceke or the rest period. They wait until two days have passed and they come back to fulfill the required seven days. At that time a new fire is built and the whole grounds put through a purification process.

Of the next period of the "busk" and the "fast" much can be written, perhaps volumes. I am not be able to do as it is extensive and esoteric. The scientists and social organizations have tried to lay bare the totality of the Indian but have failed.

To further expand on what I have written I will resort to notes I have made in brief studies of Hinduism, Buddhism etc., "to shore-up" my people's beliefs.

How can anyone attain occult powers as my people did? I quote from the Secret Doctrine: "The desire to learn. Perfect control over the passions and desires. Chastity, pure companionship; pure food, that which brings into the body none but pure influence. The frequency of a pure locality; one free from vicious taint of any kind; pure air and seclusion. He must be endowed with intelligence, that he may comprehend the principals of nature; Concentrativeness that his thoughts may be preserved from wandering and self control that he may always be master over his passions and weakness. Five things he must relinquish, ignorance, egotism, (conceit) Passion (sensual) selfishness and – fear of death." Another essential my people would add – *Fasting*.

A Creek will gather some cedar, a little of wild sage and climb a hill or go to a place of absolute seclusion. He rises at daybreak, drinks no liquids nor eats any food. A small fire is built on which is fed the cedar and sage. The swirling smoke and scent helps to do away with any distractions. He concentrates and meditates on that he desires to know. Sometimes it will be only for the day, but at other times it may take many days. Sometimes the "Little People" play tricks to get your attention, such as having a deer or some other animal approach you. The pestering is sort of a sign that you are nearing contact with the ethereal spirits.

It is a strong willed person who endures these rituals. It is known that some fasted until there was no desire for food and came near to insanity, but accomplished that which they were seeking. When they had gained power to do *good* or *evil* they would make a choice.

10

Some gained knowledge of roots and herbs and other things that had medicinal properties.

The pharmacology and material medicine of the Indian, his knowledge of roots and herbs etc., was extensive. He was well versed and knowledgeable in the science of botany. In the vast field of flora of the forests he recognized those most needed for his people. He knew and understood the materia medicine of each plant and of all other than roots and herbs. He was called the Hilishaya or doctor. The one who prognosed and diagnosed the patient was called Kerra (knower). He knew what caused the ailment and recommended a doctor.

The diagnostics of the Kerra are astounding and I can only relate an incident as an example. A baby was choking, coughing and could not spit out the phlegm – was turning blue in the face. They rushed him to a knower (whom I knew but will not mention names) whose diagnosis was like this: "the little creatures that runabout on the beachlands. . . . the blueringed hunter-wasp." The baby was rushed to the doctor. They told him what the knower said. He told them to go to the river at the old crossing where you will see little black snails on rocks above water. Touch the baby's tongue to the waters; take a snail and rub its tongue with it. Do this four days. The ailment left the child and today he is a middle aged man in good health – my cousin. He and I believe it was a case of pneumonia and he was made sick by the snails. The Creeks believe and know that animals, birds, snakes and fish and other things in nature cause sickness. If a deer has caused you to be sick a root or a plant related to that animal is used, such as in this case the deer potato. Only the Kerra (knower) and the Hilishaya (medicine man) can know the remedy. It would be useless for the Anglo medicos to try and understand the Indian's medical practice.

Chikili said that on the day the Sun Chasers were to resume the last of the "busk" Yahola appeared to the Chief and counseled him: "It has been decided by the Great Spirit that you and the people move to where you saw the marked stone on the Chatohoche river. You have done well and increased and from now on you are Cowetams; in your language – Kowetvs mahmvye. You are promised to be such a great nation that others will want your protection." With that he disappeared into the great sky.

The people in general knew only to obey and reasoned that the river Okmulgee did not produce enough water to care for the people, so willingly they marched westward to Chatahoche.

Geographically in the southeast part of the United States there lay three rivers: Alabama, Chattahoche, and Talapoosa; the fork of the Chattahoche was the Flint river. On the Okmulgee river there existed only one Creek town by that name, but later disbanded.

Today, as I look back at the history of my people it seems that the Great Spirit (God) chose this vast area as a paradise for the Muskogee tribe of Indians.

The Cowetans found the old campground on the Chatta-hoche and went about the business of laying-out a much larger square and reseated the notables in this manner: In the west arbor, or bed which had two sections north and south, were seated the Wind and Bird clan with the chief who was of the Bird clan. In the rear were seated the Bear and Beaver. In the north bed were the Blues in this order: the greater Hemeha of the Bird clan, the Blue of the Fox clan and a Hemeha of the Beaver. Hemeha, as referred to, were called the Precious ones. In the east arbor were seated women and children with the rest of the clans. (when there is no fast) In the south bed which is called the warrior's bed were seated the Panther and Potato (Kvtcha and Ahalaka) clan. The head warrior was of the Potato or Ahalakalke clan and the vice chief (Meko apoktv) was of the Panther or Kvtcha) clan. The two medicine pots were at the north end of the Chief's bed. The ball ground was at the northeast of the east arbor.

In time, as the population grew, there was need to expand and so it did into a great Confederacy. The Creek town of the Cowetans was its nucleus. There were forty towns; four on the main river of Alabama; ten on the Coosa; Thirteen on the

Tallapoosa; Eleven on the Chattachooche and two on the Flint river. Each town had its own square and the seating of its officials was very much varied. The Tokepatche square on the Talapoosa river was the most complicating and exact, probably according to Yahola's plan.

Much has been written about the religious beliefs and the medical practices of the Muskogee or Creek Indians by the Anglo-Americans, but nothing of its esoterics has been revealed by them. It would take a scholarly fullblood with a Ph.D. in ethmology, but there are none, and not likely to be any in the future.

Many generations have passed and the Sun Chasers are no more and only we the sprouts are left.

Seeds of Yahola

By the will of the wind they drift
    Some furry and bristled, others winged
                to far corners

You tell them I said this

Wandering, wandering though the woods
    by clear and swift waters.
My mind backlash of
        amorphous webs
        seeking clear thoughts —
Then abstraction came to view.
        Foetus of Dragon fly
        hanging sac of blue
        from a driftwood twig,

14

Red, silver, obsidian black,
Like dewdrop falls unfolding
            creature perfect.

The belly of earth swelling
      I ride the drum beat
            sun-fishing
            and hang on.
I hear the turtle shells'
            rhythmic beat
and the songs – the songs
            to day break.
Sunrise swallows
      pent-up feelings
      and I sleep
      – filled.

Midnight moon paints,
      in its wake,
      ripples of silvery fish,
The Loon paddles them under
      in the eerie hours,
      Man hears and thinks
      bewitching thoughts.

Spider knows nothing
            of its self –
Knows not his purpose.
He is a tool of nature
      that shows perfection
Without the spirits and
            the elements,
            there would be

                no webs
                no man;
          Just depth and darkness.

Hogs never look up to see
Where the acorns are coming from.
And too it rains on the rich
        as well as on the poor;
There's a moral in this truth,
        but never a harangue.
So my people – the red race
        dance and sing in humbleness
        directed to that Spirit on high
        our own way of looking up
    to our maker – to our giver
        of life everlasting.

The Naming Ceremony

When about twelve years old
Boys were scratched* for a name.
At the gathering of the square,*
So for me it was announced
My name would be, Wōt'Kogee*,
My grandfather wished it so.
In later years toward manhood
I was known as Wōtko Emvrv
And was seated in the north arbor.
Those were days of strenuous physical training
Depending much on strict discipline,
Rough and tough – laughing at pain.
With a mouth full of water we ran a mile
At the end we spat it out.
All through our teen years we knew not
The thrill of courtship with young women.
The marriage law was that old men marry
Young women, and young men older ones.
It had been proven for many generations
Their progeny were healthier and lived longer.

*scratched – the medicine man scratched the legs and arms
with a sharp flint until they bled.
*Square – the court square of four brush arbors.
*Wōt'Kogee – Little Racoon.
*Wōtko Emah'thla.

Rededication

Greencorn, ripe with browning silks
    marking the new year of
Sage old men of the old Creek nation
    Kowakogee, Walesa and Saba
      Lame and crutched
      Trudge to the old country
from which their ancestors were driven like cattle.
      they go to see
    That ancient paradise
    Once a land of milk and honey
They go to dedicate their lives anew
    with the ancient ones
    to see the dead raised in old haunts
    to see the great communal fields
    to hear the drum and old chants.
No river too wide or canyons too deep;
    for a fish will part the waters
    and the mind dovetail the canyon's banks
    together with a song.
Singing too on the turtle path
joining with bear and deer trails.
      The hawk seeking quail
      and the woodlands, mana
    The "little people" guiding them.
The old rock land-mark glowed
With blood blotched petroglyphs
  on their approach to Chattahoche.
Old Alibama mushroom wrinkles,
    a hundred years growth
  greets them as if but yesterday
Smelling of redroot in his blood
Sits with them in a circle
after the fast – after the medicine
    and then the quiet se'a'nce.
A low rumble in bowels of the earth

Old warrior bones sprout –
        take on flesh
tens of thousands – braves, chiefs
        brother tribes
        Euchee, Cherokee, Choctaw
        Shawnee and Chickasaw.
Old friends – Mochesoke
Katcha emathla, Tecumseh, Watashe;
Old wives, Wisey, Yana, Tooske
        and Poloke.
The gourd chimes a requiem
        red tears from the sun
        rocks moan and split
        day curtain-night curtain rent
        moon pales to naught
        winds roar without sound.
The great valley swallows its bones,
The oldmen, star showered, awaken
        to the last song of the all night dance;
        a rooster crows
        a turkey gobbles
        little yellow birds twitter
        the sunlight.

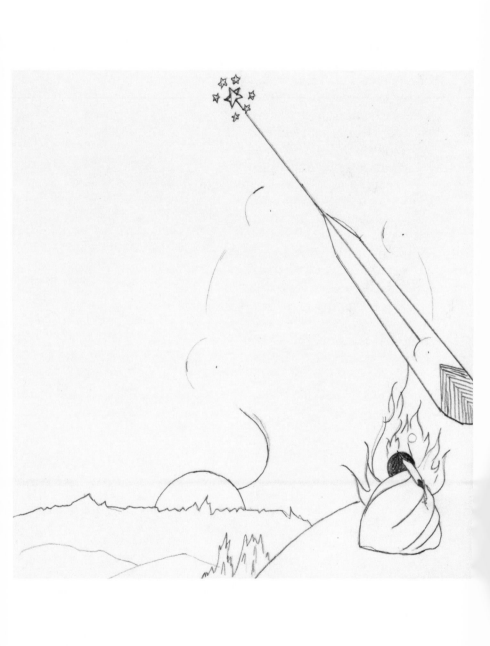

Chasers of the Sun

From out the navel of the earth
They poured like ants to chase the sun
        To its beginning.
As it arose they shot an arrow
  in its direction to keep the course.
They marched and found the arrow standing
The arrow flew to eastward again
the tribe found it and shot it again.
For many years they followed it;
  it finally fell on the banks
  of a very muddy river
  it lay pointing back to them.
Here a town was laid-out
Here they lived for many years.
The sun mystified them still.
Said the Chief: "Let's shoot the arrow
  we will chase the sun once more."
They crossed rivers, conquering tribes,
  building squares, planting their roots.
Old chiefs dies — new chiefs chase
Nation after nation the arrow flies
— then at the shores of the great white waters
  it fell pointing to the people.
Thus was the wonderment's end
  and the history of the origin
  of my people
  the Muskoke.

PART TWO:

Climbing the Mountain

Climbing the Mountain

I had this poetic urge to write something that would astound me, but it turned out to be like a very weak laxative. So, while waiting for my Muse to inspire me, I've been leafing through some old notes and suggestions. Sometimes that awakens my desire to write or sparks an idea that I jump on to like a dog on a bone. But therein lies a mystery; sometimes the dog will lie down and gnaw the bone for awhile and then leave it lay. At other times he buries it, though it be very meaty. Perhaps there's a similarity of action here and my notes are that meaty bone I buried a long time ago.

Note 1: Contemporary man although rejecting fantasy and myth aspires to make it a reality. True for man to fly was a fantasy, but he does just that now, but only mechanically. What he cannot grasp is the irrelevance of Spirit to matter. Spirit, as I use the term, is in the sense of a broad generalization. The gods, and there are many gods, rule in this other world, each self delegated with a power peculiar to its governing law. This is one group of beings (Spirits) as opposed to the Theocratic governing body which is the fountain head of pristine laws. These spiritual entities are the true governers of mankind through the ages.

Superstition in the light of modern science and religion is a fantasy, but we strive to become superhuman. Modern man in his attempt to super-intelligence, shackles himself in matter and has not the faith to shed it, therefore he still flounders in ignorance. Other civilizations found the key to separating matter from the *ethereal* or *spirit*.

Being native American and having no others blood flowing in my veins, this notation leads me to dissertate on the belief of the Indian as pertains to the ethereal and Spirits. We are often branded as superstitious and I think that is a misnomer, but rather we truly believe in the supernatural, having no fear of it. There is psychic distance between the Indian and Anglo American. The Indian is more susceptible and sensitive to non-physical forces. May I present here an extreme

25

case of the need for a non-physical force or power. My grandmother told me this, which happened during the forced migration of my people, the Muskogee or Creeks, from their homeland. A small group of her Clan were being led by their medicine man when they came to the rim of a steep and rocky canyon. A light snow was falling. Three or four days before, they were traveling with one wagon, a team of horses and a small supply of cornmeal and dried meat. A group of mounted ruffians, claiming to be the United States Cavalry, caught up with them and confiscated all they had.

Their leader (the medicine man) gathered them around a small fire, (they dared not build a large fire for fear of revealing their whereabouts) and as night approached they seemed to have been in a trance. He told them, "We cannot afford to go to the head of the canyon, but in order to escape other marauders we must cross here." She said it seemed that the canyon banks came together and they crossed over safely.

To substantiate this miracle a retired officer of the United States Cavalry wrote a book of his experiences mentioning the disappearance of the group, which they never caught up with nor ever found, even a trace of them.

Someone wrote this: "The Divinity of the Great Spirit is frequently illustrated by reference to His miracles and to the supernormal which he so often evidenced. Supernormal powers are of themselves no evidence of divinity at all.

Great exponents of evil can perform the same miracles and demonstrate the same capacity to create and to transcend the normal faculties of man."

I am thankful to the philologists, anthropologists, archaeologists, ethnomusicologists and the whole of Anglo scientific scholars for their final determination that the native American imagistic whole is of a mythic entelechy – a numinous thing, beyond our intelligence.

2nd Note: "To obtain occult powers, these essentials are: A desire to learn. Perfect control over the passions and desires. Chastity; pure companionship; pure food; that which brings into the body none but pure influences; the frequenting of a pure locality; one free from vicious taint of any kind; pure air and seclusion. He must be endowed with intelligence, that he may comprehend the principals of nature; Concentrativeness, that his thoughts may be prevented from wandering; and self control that he may always be master over his passions and weakness.

Five things he must relinquish – ignorance, egotism, (Conceit) Passion (sensual), Selfishness and fear of death." (Quote from the Secret Doctrine.)

These are the things that the Indian Shaman or prophet practiced and conquered thereby obtaining supernatural powers. I with only a very meagre education, no degrees, not much schooling, but spent years as a transient, then settled down and had an urge to write in my old age. My grandmother taught me songs to sing over roots and herbs made into a tea. She taught me how to pray or meditate in the Indian way on things I so desired. So I climbed a certain mountain here to rendezvous with the "Little people" or the ethereal spirits.

It is a day I fast; take in no liquids or food. As I climb I begin concentrating on what my desire will be. I reach the top and survey my surroundings. It is quiet and peaceful and the air washed clean and purified by the ozone. There are tall pines and cedars. I build a small fire and lay sprigs of cedars on it occasionally. I sit before it and study the flames and smell the burning cedar – I face the east.

There were times a deer would stand close by and stare. Wild animals do not distract one's thoughts. I prayed or concentrated on my wish and hope to be able to write, on these trips to the mountain top. It took me three trips before I could isolate all outside thoughts and saw only myself composing poetry and prose though they seemed nonsensical; varied subjects and objects were presented. Divine afflatus often occurs at this time. It seems the one theme that stood out in my mind went something like this: "I am earth in part – I belong to the earth. All of Creation is of the elements and shall return to it."

So to conclude my dissertation on that one notation I dare say that one (if he be Indian) chooses a hill or a mountain top to shed worldly evils as he climbs, he figuratively sheds his clothing, piece by piece, to stand naked before the supernatural to come in cosmic unity with it.

There is an ocean of difference of how the Indian practices expanding the mind or being "turned on" as compared to the "now generation" of the Anglo-American's. As it is well known now that generation turned to the use of hallucinogens such as marijuana, L.S.D., D.M.T. and Psilocybin. Together and along with such, there is in their kind of music that is narcotizing. Its lyrics, atonal and abstract sounds produce psychedela or intoxication of sorts. It is possibly true that the disjointing of the mind from the physical structure may lead to permanent separation.

So – to what avail, to what advantage has it been that I climbed that mountain and prayed in my Indian way, for expansion of my mind; to be able to recall past knowledge and experiences that are recorded in the files and indexes of my brain?

I had never given a thought to the possibilities of my writing prose, poetry, the history of my people or of the Native American in general. Then I attended my first Conference of Native American writers. I felt very much out of place when I learned that those Indians of various tribes were professionals in the field of writing. Some were editors and publishers of widely circulated books and magazines pertaining to Indian culture, tradition and religions. I was very much impressed by their urging that the Indian must write as a survival tactic. When they returned to their respective homes and businesses I received from them so much material and chapbooks by other writers, that I was overwhelmed and very much inspired to write.

I was amazed at the proficiency of those native American writers of prose and poetry in the various anthologies and individual books. I dare to say that given the chance, the Indian proves to be equally intelligent to the Anglo American. The only difference in our perspective seems to be as Paula Gunn Allen stated, "Native American literature and Western literature are hardly compatible. Basic assumptions about the universe are not the same."

So, after much study of the facts, I began to prepare a manuscript of what I knew about my people. I did not have to do any research or spend time in libraries. In this instance I recalled the days my grandmother used to send me to the spring for buckets of water; a chore I hated. I was just an ornery "snotty-nosed-kid," as the white folks used to say of their own. We had a name for that spring which is in our language: "Wekiyhonecha" which means; "wild water" or "wild well." At the time, I could see nothing strange or mysterious about the spring, until my grandmother asked me one day: "Have you seen a snake in the spring?" My answer was "no" but there was a slight chilling sensation up and down my spine. To make matters worse, she said; "If you ever see one with a single horn on its head, you let me know." She went about her business with a brush broom, sweeping the yard. I stood watching her with many questions in my mind, and she seemed to have read them when she said: "There are snakes which we call 'Cheto-yapehaya' that live in certain wild springs, they are wanted by the medicine man (Kethla) for their horns, which have much power to be used in many ways. You must not tell this to any white person." I answered: "Omiyvkos," I will not tell.

This happened seventy years ago and in that lapse of time I learned more about it and wrote a bi-lingual book, called *The Horned Snake*. I only had one short poem in the book concerning the snake. The myth about it is as mysterious as that of the Loch Ness Monster. I explained that the horn was always in the possession of the medicine man or Kethla, who was sort of like a monk who was retired to asceticism. What I know about it is merely from "hear-say," but a man or a warrior in battle could be made impervious to missiles of war by the use of, or being doctored with, the horn by the medicine man.

I am of a poor Indian family who lived practically on the banks of the Arkansas river. There were about twenty Indian families in the surrounding area who had settled there after the Civil War. Our association with each other was truly a brotherhood calling ourselves of "One Fire." If at the time it could have been called corporate, then our town was named Koweta. Being orphaned when I was about a year old, I lived part time with my aunt and uncle in another town called Okfuskee seventy miles away. Here I was indoctrinated into the mysteries of Indian superstitions, traditions and religion. At a certain age, Indian boys were "scratched" by one whose responsibility it was to do that. The scratching instrument (if it could be called that) was a sliver of flint. The calves of our legs were scratched up and down, a shallow cut, drawing little blood. We were marked forever.

I must set the stage here for the peculiarities of social behavior of my people. We lived within the perimeter of about four square miles where an ancient civilization had left its marks. The Deepfork River snaked its way through those deep dark woods, washing down stream silt and loam for thousands of years, revealing great layers of sandstone slabs.

Our loghouse sat on the benchland of the river which lay about a mile and a half north. To the west of us, for about a quarter of a mile, the ledges of rocks ended. One large slab tablerock probably $8' \times 10' \times 6'$, was outstanding in that a conical hole about 12" in diameter and 12" deep had been ground out away from the edge about three feet. There was another like it on the banks of the river. For grinding or braying corn we used a pestle and mortar made of wood. The mystery of it lies in the fact that no pestle for the rock mortar has ever been found. To add another mystery to that rock-table, (preturnatural) on misty dark evenings, or dusk, an apparition was seen of an Indian woman standing on it.

Before section lines were ever surveyed the old Indian trail passed by our house and the Table-rock, then trailed down into the river bottoms, crossing the river. It was known as the "old Indian crossing;" (Tiyketa Liska). I was always told to never wander beyond this crossing because the "little people" lived there and they might entice you into the great bottoms and you would be lost—maybe forever. I remember an incident that happened that involved those elfin sprites. Everybody knew old lady Pologie who was nearing the century mark in age. She lived alone in a one room log house which was near her grandchildren's framed house. She had been bedridden for almost a year and could not walk. No one knew what her ailment was and took for granted she would die from old age.

Her brother, Ak-kowe, in making his usual visits found her gone one day and in alarm spread the word. A search party went into the dark river bottoms and found her about a mile from her cabin. She surprised her rescuers in that she could walk with some assistance. When they got her to her bed she told them that the little people ('ste'lopuchkoge) came to her bed—a lot of them. They danced at the foot of her bed, singing songs that she knew. They were jolly and happy and she felt happy with them. She said they took her by the hands and enticed her to go with them to the woods. Three days afterwards, she passed away.

Again, a young man went hunting for squirrels in about the same area that Pologie was found, but deeper in the woods. A day and a half had passed before the community missed him. A search party spread out in the bottoms and found him wandering about seemingly in a daze. I knew Wiley to be strong and healthy and he knew those bottoms well, but here was his story: "I saw something crouched like an animal, it was quite a ways from me. I nocked my best arrow and approached it in a crouch. When I came in full view of it I realized it was a giant snake, one that I had never seen before.

32

It was coiled and ready to strike. Its head was hideous and its eyes were locked on mine. I could not draw my bow because I was trembling and losing strength. It was drawing me to him. With the last ounce of strength and breath I whooped at the top of my voice – turned and ran. Though I was running free and away I could still feel his hypnotic pull. I'm glad to see you all but I don't know what is the matter with me – I have a headache and everything seems to be going around and around."

The search party led him out of the woods and turned him over to the medicine man. It took many moons of "doctoring" to bring Wiley's senses back to normal. Though many hunters searched those wooded bottoms, the snake was never found.

As a young man I had hunted in those bottoms with no fear, but remembering Wiley's experience. Once I was looking for wild "Possum" grapes when I discovered something unusual in the fork of an elm tree. It was whitish and embedded deep. At first I thought it was an arrow head and was about to try and dig it out – but something "stayed" my hands. There was something mysterious about it as the sap of the tree was "brownish" that drained down from it. When I returned home I told my uncle about it and he said that it was a "madstone" put there by a medicine man a long time ago. He explained that the insane were treated with it to bring back sanity. He told me that in one in a thousand deer is found the object called "madstone."

Now to continue relating the mysticisms (and there were many) surrounding my people I can vouch for the following: My aunt was what may be termed a seeress and she seemed to me as very odd. At times, I remember, she would shovel some coals out of the fireplace and lay green cedars on it until it began to smoke. She smoked each room and ended in circling the house with it. She explained to us (children) that evil spirits were attempting to enter the house and the cedar smoke would keep them away. I had been away visiting my grandmother in Koweta for some time, when at bedtime she brought a pistol and put it under my pillow. She explained that a "Sleep maker" (Nociychka haya) was known to be entering homes to do evil things. She further explained that I being a stranger with a pistol, he would know that, and not bother us. Otherwise we would all be put to sleep until sunrise. The only way we would know he had been here is the scratch he makes on our arms or legs.

There were many ways that a person who had attained power would use it for good or evil. My aunt and my grandmother were experts in the knowledge of medicinal roots and herbs or, to put it in a more sophisticated sense, materia medica and therapeutics. The secret in preparing a concoction was in knowing the proper song or prayers blown upon it. My aunt had a small iron pot and a hollow cane or reed with which she practiced her profession.

The Sleep Maker (Nocichka Haya)

In Taskigi I was born,
   wrenched from the womb
   — an evil spawn — nocturnal
   named — "Coon walking in the night."
Denied pap for stronger meats,
   roasted hearts of Mockingbirds,
   raw melt of Deer
   Stewed tortoise in the shell —
      bland-saltless

Natural sugar from the belly
      of the Bumblebee;
Sired by Ho-dul-gul-gi
      of the Wind clan
      mothered by her kindred
      of the 'Coon Clan.

My endowment of this union,
   power to make sleep of one
   or as many as I choose.
By edict of the powers
   of the evil ones
I lived in the endless bottoms
   of the River, Deep Fork.

August moon still in slumber
   behind a curtain of velvet black.
To my house of logs
   the "Little People" came
   some old and gray, but spry.
they said: "We give you eyes
      of the Tiger moth"
I begged to have his coiled tongue.
   "Yes that" they said.

"and this cup of Hell's black drink
to ward off Saint's retributive justice."

2

They pointed and crooked a finger
        in ridicule, saying:
"We know of your plan of seduction
upon the object of your love
        of the Bird clan."
I shouted: "I will strike you with
    fire – Ah-wa-has!" (begone!)
and they disappeared.

Ayee hah! I'm frightened
        of my visage;
    the livid scar across my face
    from the claws of bear;
    Long hair – black and coarse
    a peculiar tic of spitting
        uncontrolled,
    walking fast – like Fox trot
        head down.
Barefoot, pants
        frayed,
    smelling of wolf and Coyote.

Never seen by day
    feared by men
    shunned by women.
She – my love imprisoned
    by taboos – sheltered
    from men – growing old
    Not knowing motherhood.
    sweet-warm, soft voiced.

3

The moon rises fluorescent – exposing
long black shadows, latticed, wierd,
The mole cricket starts his constant
    Low whirring whistle.
The great horned owl, the harbinger
    of evil and good, sounds
    a muffled summons
    endearing to my cult.

As the moon grows,
    I emerge accordingly
    a new creature.
I can feel it – the transfiguration;
The mood is set – all signs are concordant.
I will ply my trade.
    "A fire! – a fire!" the little people shouted
    "We'll dance the Gar dance
    and send you on your way!"
In my medicine bundle I felt
    the flint-needle sharp
    es sap ka, it is called.
They were singing:
    "We-hey-hayo-neh – "
Funereal – doleful.
Beyond the pale – in dark shadows
        wolves' eyes blinked yellow
        halo-sahgada, the cottonmouth
        King of water snakes arouses;
A screech owl dives, snapping
making sounds like a child
        being throttled.
High moon now – I must accomplish
        what I'm driven
            To.

Spiritual Renewal

The fire, the medicine, the Turtleshells
  The dancers and the songs
Terminating fasting and feasting
  Until the break of day.
Shadows eat away the sunlight
The darkness of the night
   giving birth
To the light from the fire.
The morning sun revealing the
Mystic circle, the invisible wall
Surrounding the whole of Indian beliefs
. . . their hopes and prayers rise with smoke
  a savor to the Great Spirit.
From out of the circle they all leave
   weak from loss of sleep,
   but feeling the newness of the soul
Like an infant's first sight of light
All the world awakens anew
   for them.

Indian Epicure

My body full of medicine
Sweat-fumes of roots and herbs
Early morn a plunge in the river
I emerge a new man.
Este Maskoke toyis eha!*
In the wildwoods Indian fire
Great chunks of redeyed coals
Blinking eyes with white ashes.
The Sowee Sowee* are out
The smoke of Blackjack and Red oak
A soothing and calming of the soul.
My cup is filled and running over
Is my dominating thought.
I hear the women shaking shells
the rhythmic sound of Saka! Saka*!
I smell the roasting Buffalo hump
and a side of Venison.
Boiling corn in the husk
Pumpkin and squash to eat with honey
wild grape dumplings and Chatta haga*
A great pan of Sour Cornbread.
. . . a mug of O'Sofkee.*
So; my people fared well.

*I am a Muskogee Indian!
*Jar fly
*Saka Saka-Saka Saka—turtle shells of gravel being shook
*Cornmeal blued with burnt pea hulls patted and boiled
*Corngrits cooked with wood-ash lye allowed to sour slightly

Powers To Be Had

Acculturated, I speak English
      so my people disown me.
I chose the power to be unseen
Hicka Seko it is called;
      through self-inflicted starvation
No food, no water, for days and days
      of soul searing mediations
      to near insanity the fourth day.
These distractions have gone away;
      the snooping deer, the scolding jay
. . . Thoughts – thoughts inconsequential,
      voices, voices urging me
to take the power of the elements
      that can open safes in banks
      with just a puff of my breath
      point my finger and a person dies.
Those were powers of the devil.
I had a choice and was urged
      to do good or do evil.
I wrestled with the psychic forces
      . . . drained myself and fell asleep.

Mind Over Matter

My old grandmother, Tekapay'cha
   stuck an ax into a stump
   and diverted a tornado.
In minutes we would have been destroyed.
It struck the little town of Porter
   ripping up the railroad tracks,
   twisted the rails and stood them up.
There was power in that twister.
There was power in my grandmother.
Those who doubt, let them doubt.

Where Fairies Live

I was ten or twelve then —
With my little bow and arrows;
I was told not to go
Into the deep dark bottoms
Of the legendary Deep Fork
   "You might see little people"
They said: "and you won't live very long."
My grandfather told me where they lived;
   on trees that had growth of limbs
— like hair and quills on Porcupine.
Curiosity tingled my being,
but something kept me from the bottoms.
Instead — I watched a crayfish digging
   a well to store his needed water:
   up he'd come with little mud balls
   building a tower around the hole.
I'll see how long I'm going to live:
   So I started counting the balls.
   "No! — this is wrong" I said.
"I know I'll live long enough —
   I didn't see the little people."

The Square of the Kowetas (Kawet'vlke)

June 24, 1987

Of that which is natural
      is the key to our belief.
Strike the flint – rub the wood
      to create fire was the law.
Look to the sun and moon
      which without there's no life.
Four is our sacred number
      so the arbors are that many
On the square – star measured;
      east, west, north and south
Make the trees fall eastward
      Trim the limbs for the arbors,
Set up the pole – the sacred one
      which is called Pok'Kabe*
and was carried by four men
      to the mystery hole prepared;
At the top, the Buffalo Skull.

*a tall pole for stick ball games, etc.

43

A Full Cup and More

August 5, 1987

In the shade of my brush arbor
     leaning on my walking stick
     chin on hands – deep think.
Yonder my old lady pounding corn
Yonder hanging side of deer
Yonder hanging drying pumpkins
My pouch is full of wild tobacco.
My cup is full and running over.
Many sons, many daughters,
Children happy everywhere.
I can see many arbors
Each with fire from my coals.
Sickness or hunger never here,
Woods full of deer and bear,
Rivers and streams full of fish
My cup is always full and
     running over.
I say to Great Spirit:
     Mah″Tooooo!*

*Thank you.

Medicare

(No strings attached)

Asthmatic and wheezing I tromped
through sandburrs and bullnettles,
white sandy soils—hot winds.
Weaved through postoak runners
      —sawtooth briars.
Stopped to rest and smoke a Camel.
Like a fugitive from the law
bypassing the clear clean roads,
            Why?
I'm a fullblooded Indian—that
            is why.
I'm going to see old Nokose
   for him to diagnose my illness.
He lives in an old and sturdy
            cabin of oak logs.
Two big Indian dogs came out
            to sniff me over.
Though their hackles are up they never
            bark.
They are a part of the mysticism
            of their owner,
and their scrutiny of a stranger
            is conveyed.
There is a rapport twixt Indian and Indian
      . . . no lengthy conversations, just
            presence and silence.
Finally old Nokose began
to relate the cause of my
            illness.
Humped and seeming in a trance
he spoke of entities in the spirit
            world:
The slimeless snail, the legless ant

the microscopic demons
the little blue-winged hunter
wasp.
Much beyond my understanding.
He arose and went to his
backroom
I could hear him singing in
a monotone.
I expected to smell an odor
of wild beasts,
but there was a pleasant, medicinal
whiff of mint, sage and cedar.
A white feather hung from a joist
in the center of the room
creating a mystifying air.
Old Nokose shuffled back
looked to the feather and said:
"If my diagnosis has been
right
You will turn in approval."
It seemed so long before it moved
— twisting, slowly around.
He handed me a sheaf of herbs
a tiny box of yellow dust.
Early morning for four weeks
I did as he told me.
I breathe freely with no pain
. . . and for some mysterious reason
my desire to smoke is dead.
I can say I owe the man
my life,
but would he take any money?
NO!

46

Snow Bath

All through the silent night, the snow,
   angel feathers, fell – whispering,
covering the trees of cedar and pine,
with soft white furry coats;
Redhaw berries peeking out
   from under lacy white bonnets;
Dark shadows in the brook
   like squirming, twisting dragons.
Oh, such a stillness and peace,
   but for the crunch of my steps.
I go to visit my grandfather
   taking with me his favorite drink,
   aged old Indian parched corn.
I see his cabin's faint blue smoke,
   and he – a hundred years old out taking
      his snow bath, bare to his waist
. . . shouting: "Ka'ho, ho ho'-ho!"

March, '85

47

The Mystic Fire

An old and wrinkled Indian,
Hodulgee Emathla of Okchiye town
trudged along a dusty path
carefully guarding an urn
        to his chest.
Suddenly confronting him was
his age old antagonist
        a white man.
Said he to the Indian:
        "I've been watching you
        and would like to know
        what is in that pot?"
The old man raised his hand
        his usual gesture of peace
        and explained, most humbly:
        "It contains our everlasting fire."
"Fire!" exclaimed the dense and physical.
Said the fire philosopher:
        "I take to land of Buffalo,
        the promised land of my people.
        There will kindle new fire with old."
The terrestial phantom laughed
    with maniacal hysteria
. . . slapped the ancient urn to
            the ground,
    smashing it to bits.
"Just as I thought" said the white man.
"You Indians are superstitious pagans
—now see if you can pick up
        your so called fire!"
Thereupon they parted
        neither looking back.

48

Curiosity got the better of the antagonist,
    who turned to see the Indian
    trudging away, clasping
    the whole urn to his chest.

PART THREE:

Creek Indian Humor

Native American Wit and Humor

No man that walks this earth is without that sense of the ludicrous or Comicality. If there is, then he is dead while he is alive. Perhaps it could be said that 99% of mankind is made up of caprice; whim; fancy and freakish actions. Sometimes I think that my people the Muskogee or Creeks are 100% that. I know that other tribes have their local clowns who arouse much laughter by their antics and freakish actions. We the Creeks do not have professional clowns, but every man is a clown unto himself, verbally. In my young days I attended several Indian Church gatherings and noticed that at certain "breaks" in the affairs of the church, the Preachers gathered off to themselves to tell jokes. Supposedly, they were discussing religious problems, but we boys snooped around and found out the truth. Why would they be telling jokes – these staunch Christians, these puritan hearts and above all – preachers? I suppose after the tedium of hours upon hours of preaching and teaching, the soul needed to be assuaged. So, in this case, humor was the medication.

I have come to the conclusion that no matter who you are and in what station of life whether the President of these United States, Congressman, big business "mogul" or whatever, you cannot be serious for long as humor will creep in to soothe the weary mind. I have even noticed a faint smile on the face of a "bigshot" politbureau official – humor is there too.

Hilarity to the extent that it brings tears is next to being harmful and there are those humorists who can do that. There are those who can bring out a laugh from the untouchables, the staid old officials in the Pentagon, and Will Rogers did just that. Now it must be noted here that Will was an exceptional Indian who rubbed elbows with the elite, the bourgeois and capitalistic herd, not because he was one of them, but he was expertise in revealing to them their kind of humor – the sophisticated kind that hurts, but is painless. Of course he did not tell Indian jokes that are typical of Native Americans. So, scaling this thought down to the Creek Indian jokes would be like washing your feet with your socks on. They are good at finding something funny in every little thing, no matter how insignificant, or crass.

How to put this into perspective I don't know, but it was spring and the wild onions were up big enough to gather. Saturday and the Indians were in town to supply their cupboards. One Indian stood on the street corner just looking at the traffic and passers. He had eaten a good dish of wild onions at home. A friend came up to him and noticed a piece or a "blade" of onion on his teeth. Said the friend: "Are the onions up pretty good?" With a broad grin he simply answered: "I don't know." Was that the punch line? Where is the joke? Such as that the Creeks consider to be funny. They cannot discuss any serious matters without allowing humor to intervene. It is known that in the old days in Creek court sessions and trials the questioning by lawyers and interpretations by interpreters brought on much roaring laughter.

So where ever the Creeks meet, whether in twos, fours or a crowd, there will be chuckles, laughter and at times roaring laughter. There may be an old stonefaced Creek leaning on his cane as people pass by. Be assured he is smiling inwardly of something funny that he saw. When he tells it to his friends, there will be, in unison, a thunderous roar of laughter.

August 9, '84

Yellow Cat Incident

The Okfuske Creek women are a stout lot, the younger generation being tall, lanky and of a complexion without blemish. There were more old maids than usual, but a woman at forty or even at fifty years was considered young. May be that there was a shortage of eligible males that the situation was as it was.

There was a gathering at a house where some kind of activity was going on such as peach peeling or pecan gathering and families came to to help out. At any rate it was a good time for the "old maids" to show-off their physique — their whatever it is that charms a man.

Food had been prepared and it was time to "set the table," so to speak. One of the oldest of the maids was known as Hattka, who at this minute was aware of the men folks sitting and watching every move the women made. She decided to make herself more active than the others. She tip-toed, pranced and swayed from kitchen to dining table, putting dishes of things in their proper places. She was putting on a show of grace and beauty to prove to the men that she was without fault. There were two others who were helping with the placing of various dishes and food. While Hattka was in the kitchen, a whole boiled pumpkin had been placed in the center of the table. There was a variety of yellow pumpkin that the Creeks raised and prepared it that way. Hattka came prancing towards the table and saw the yellow pumpkin — she stopped suddenly with raised hands, shouting: "Oh that crazy yellow cat — get off that table! Get off!" She slapped that scalding hot pumpkin and it splattered all over everything on the table.

The men turned their heads and snickered.

The Cold Nosed Dog

It was December and the thermometer hovered around zero, but that did not deter those old 'coon hunters from gathering at the country store which was also the post office. The store owner had the old box heater roaring with fire and the old timers were warm and comfortable. Sam Blackbird was there, the only Creek Indian whom they all know to be very talkative though he mangled the English language pretty bad.

Not much was being said while they were waiting for the mail carrier to arrive. Usually it was something of a political nature that would stir the fire in these old codgers. Sam Blackbird broke the "ice" by saying: "Hey! you old farts, you know I got old Saylo my dog, he got cold nose, he trail old 'coon tracks—even five days old—you know that!"

Old man Pohfal spat a gob of tobacco juice into the ash pan and replied: "No Sam, we don't know that." Sam could never pronounce that old white man's name so he called him "Poor-folks," and ever since then everybody called that family that. Another old spit and whitler spoke up. "Now Sam looka here, we all got good 'coon hounds with cold noses and you know and we know they ain't no such a dog can trail a track that old." Sam stood up and pointed a finger at all of them and began to get firey, like a Philadelphia lawyer trying to prove his case. "I can prove. . . I can prove, you got chicken or hog— I'll bet with you. . . I can prove!" They all knew that Sam was not an Indian you could joust with or argue with too long. Old man Pohfal asked: "How ya gonna prove all this?" Sam replied: "You want me prove! alright—who want go with me tonight—you poorfolks, you go with me—or anybody—I honest Injun as you say—I can prove!"

So the deal was made and at around nine o'clock that night Sam took the coaloil lantern and Pohfal the ax. They whistled for old Saylo and he was more than ready to go. This country was very rugged around Black Fox hollow and Lougard hollow. They headed up from Blackjack flats and weaved their way down to the Illinois river. The night was not too dark on account of a little moon light, but it was miserably cold.

The two hunters at first walked very briskly to keep warm though Sam had on a sheepskin coat and Pohfal an old Khaki army overcoat. They had walked for about a half an hour and old Saylo had not made a sound. They were nearing Black Fox hollow when they stopped to listen. Pohfal reached in his side pocket and got a wad of loose-leaf long-green tobacco and stuffed it in his mouth, coughed a little on account of some tobacco dust in his throat. Sam didn't use tobacco, but he sneaked a half pint of wildcat whiskey and took a nip. Pohfal said: "Looks to me like they'd be a lot of cold tracks here that your dog could have picked up by now — you don't think he could 'uv gone back home do ye?" Sam said: "That bad joke, Poor-folks, old Saylo know what he's doing." No sooner than he said that, Saylo let out a long drawn bawl that resounded from one side of the hollow to the other. That built up confidence in both of them and now they didn't feel the cold so bad. They would not move until they heard old Saylo again. Pohfal was suggesting they build a fire when the old dog opened up again, but almost out of hearing distance. Sam mentally pin-pointed the sound as north on the flats toward Lougard hollow. They scrambled down the side of Black Fox and up the other side. With all the exertion of falling, getting up, huffing and puffing, they felt the sweat under their arm pits.

By the time they reached the top and sat down to rest a little, old Saylo bawled again, but sounded as if he was coming towards them. Sam thought he was headed towards the river, to which Pohfal agreed. Saylo was not on a hot trail, they both knew that. Now that the body had cooled down they decided to build a fire. The sky was clear and Sam pointed out the Little Dipper and fixed the time to be around one o'clock in the morning. They had just got comfortable and old Saylo let out a short bawl and they both said, he's down by the river. Sam got up and said "You pee on the fire and let's go." They walked a little faster and came to the ridge that

57

overlooked the river. Saylo was bawling a little closer together, but they couldn't place where he was. They took the old goat trail down from the ridge and were within a hundred yards of the river. Old Pohfal began to have doubts about this hunt, but agreed to tough it out. They came to the river which was frozen over to six inches thick. Sam held the lantern up to see further out and there was Saylo walking around in circles sniffing the ice and bawling. Right then the old man Pohfal was about to give up saying: "Sam, dang it! There's something wrong here, he can't be smelling coon tracks on this ice and you know that." Sam countered: "I told all of you I have the coldest nosed dog around here and I can prove it. My dog Saylo never lie. If he say 'coon out there, then, 'coon is out there." About that time old Saylo let out a hot trail bawl, but he was on the other side of the frozen river. Of course Sam was a bit skeptical himself so he would lower the lantern on the ice to see if there were even signs of tracks. They both got down on their knees for a close examination and sure enough there were tracks just about two inches below the surface, big 'coon tracks. Pohfal raised up slowly saying in disbelief; "I'll be danged.!" As if he were laughing, Saylo let out three long resounding bawls. In the mind of Pohfal there was suspicion. It could be that Sam and Saylo were in cahoots with each other. These Creek Indians are a queer lot and are not to be trusted, he thought.

While the two hunters were standing non-plussed at the situation, Saylo barked "treed" meaning he had found the tree the 'coon is in. Sam and Pohfal forgot their old age and weariness and began to trot to the tree – a great water oak. Saylo was sitting on his haunches wagging his tail and barking. Sam raised the lantern high to try and spot the 'coon's eyes. He searched all through the limbs of the tree, but there were no shining eyes to be seen. Saylo, like a good 'coon dog is supposed to do, trailed wide around the tree to be sure the 'coon had not jumped out of the tree. Pohfal blowed his top: "Dammit Sam, I'm tired of this crazy hunt, they ain't no coon up that tree, you done seen they ain't, and if you aim to chop the tree down – by god I'm goin' home!" Sam, in order to calm his pardner down, handed him the bottle of whiskey and said he would chop the tree down. He took the ax and began chopping. Saylo whimpered and whined with possibly a glint in his eye. After about thirty minutes of hard chopping, Sam sat down to rest. The bottle was passed to Pohfal.

Pohfal weakened and both men took turns at chopping and the tree fell with a "whump." Immediately old Saylo jumped up on it and began to sniff all up and down it. At times he would bark, bawl and scratch at different places on the body of the tree. With some doubt and consternation the hunters examined those places. Down towards the trunk of the water oak there was a crack about an inch wide that Saylo had scratched the bark away from. Well, nothing would do for Sam but to chop a hole in the crack. It was not big enough, so he chopped a larger hole out and found that the tree was hollow. They both looked into it with the lantern and sure enough and beyond a doubt there lay the skeleton of a 'coon.

Che'noski's Fishing Story

Che'noski, fullblood Creek Indian, crippled in the Vietnam war, gets disability checks and food stamps. At times he was overcome with manic depression, but mostly he was a jolly sort of a person full of jokes. He traded his food stamps for "moonshine" whiskey and lived near the Deepfork river. He told his friends that it was a hot, humid day in August when he decided to go fishing. The ground was too dry and hard to dig for worms and there were no grasshoppers. In fact, he said he didn't know what to use for bait. He took the chance of finding something on the way to the river. He stuck a pint of "moonshine" in his hip pocket. Halfway to the fishing hole he stopped for meditation (the Indians' way with a hunter's song.) A few steps down the trail there lay a water moccasin with a spring frog in its mouth. Quickly, he stepped on the snake and took the frog from his mouth. Still standing on the snake he put the frog in his pocket. The snake with mouth wide open was struggling to get loose. He thought to himself — I wonder what he would do if I poured some whiskey down his throat. So he did that and it thrashed wildly through the weeds and out of sight. He said he gave a little belly laugh and went on down to the river. He hooked the frog under the skin of its back and sailed it away out in deep water. He took a good nip out of his bottle and sat down comfortably hoping for a bite. He had not sat there very long when he felt a nudge at his back. He twisted around to see and to his surprise, there was that same snake with a frog in its mouth.

An Indian Dog

Che'coni was a large and typical Indian dog that knew only Indian (Creek) commands. . . and smart. His owner was astounded at his intelligence, though a little late in finding it out. What started his attention to it was when one morning he decided to go squirrel hunting and as always Che'coni (he called him Che for short) would jump up on him, make a circle and take off. He (his master) had taken down his old .22 rifle, Che sniffed it and ran to the wooded area. The question of how the dog knew that with that gun he hunted squirrels ran through his mind. He had seen Che do things beyond the logical reasoning of ordinary dogs and times he scratched his head in wonderment.

The next day he decided to put Che to a test so got his double barreled shot gun and stood on the porch. Che came around the house, jumped up on him, made two quick circles and headed for open ground where the corn and oats were. He knew that his master was going quail hunting. What perplexed his master was that he never ever used him to hunt birds as the dog was not a bird dog.

All night, that night, his master rolled and tumbled thinking about how he could put Che to a real test, one that would prove to him that it was sort of an accident. So, early that morning he got his fishing pole and stepped out on the porch and waited for Che to come bouncing up. He didn't show so he called him and whistled for him, but no Che. "Just as I thought" he said and started across the barn lot on his way to the river. Just as he turned around the corner of the barn, his eyes nearly popped out at what he saw. There was Che, digging as fast as he could after worms.

61

Old Squirrel Hunter

Oldman Choska nearing ninety years, still hunted squirrels in the Deepfork bottoms. His favorite squirrel dog was much older than he and old age had crippled him. He was blind and afflicted with ailments akin to old dogs. He would whimper and whine while seemingly looking towards the bottoms and Choska knew he wanted to go hunting. Out of pity and sorrow for him he would lay some straw in a wheel barrow with a quilt over it. He would gently pick up his old dog and lay him on the padded wheelbarrow. He would wheel him through the woods and it seemed his hunting pardner gained new life and became spirited as he sniffed the air and pointed his nose in the direction his owner should take him. He had not lost his sense of smell and was very accurate in pointing out the tree the squirrel would be in. When the old man shot and their prey fell, the dog would try to get up and though very weakly he would bark with joy. Thusly they wheeled home with two or three fat squirrels.

Baseball Game

Other than playing their usual "stickball" game on Sunday afternoons the Creek Indians had marked off a baseball diamond away back in the sticks, so to speak. They were poor financially and could not afford the usual equipment for the game, so they only had one ball and a bat. They had played with this one ball so many times that the covering was frayed and ripped and sewn and resewed many times; even the color looked like dry cow dung.

There had been some boasting by the pitcher that he would "fan" every one out there, and he had, until old Pokonafka stepped in to bat. He was a big heavyset beer bellied Indian with a smirk on his face always. He let two strikes go by, but on the third pitch he hit that ball so hard that while it was high over center field the covering came off and began to float down. The center fielder picked the covering up and acted like he was going to throw it to home plate. The ball itself was never found.

Caught Red Handed

Most of the Creek Indians raised hogs, cattle and chickens, but there were those that were allergic to hard work – such as the hog thieves. In this case there was Sokha and Elecha, experts at stealing hogs. Right at this moment they were after a fat barrow on the flats. They chased it for a hundred yards, or so, until it took a pig trail into a steep hollow. They were right on it and despite their hold of a leg and ears and all the squealing – it got loose and took up the side of the hollow. There was a wild scramble for beast and man over sawtooth briars and rolling rocks. Old Sokha was right on it near the top rim of the hollow and Elecha right behind him. Just as all three appeared at the top, huffing and puffing, the owner of the hog was standing there. With some quick thinking, old Sokha was pointing up at a tall hickory tree, saying: "I know he up there 'cause I saw him run up tree!" Elecha craned his neck up and down the tree and was pointing when the owner said: "No – he didn't go up that tree – he went home because it was my hog."

Hotdog Question

There was a Carnival in a small town in Indian Country. Two old and wrinkled Creeks decided to see what it was all about. As they walked and gawked down the midway they noticed a large sign advertising Hotdogs. The aroma of pickles and frying onions aroused their appetites so that they bought a hotdog sandwich apiece. One parted the sandwich and in suspicion said to his friend: "I wonder what part of the dog this is?"

Free Loaders

Old Kemo, an Indian friend of mine, learned the art of making whiskey from his white neighbors and had what is called mash, in a barrel. He lived on the prairie, so hid the barrel just over a long ridge. The day came for him to inspect the stuff to see if it was ready to be distilled. Just as he got near it a blackbird flew up from the rim of the barrel. He sat down in wonderment as the bird flew over the ridge and out of sight. He gave it no further thought. In about five minutes the bird came back, took a nip of beer and flew over the ridge. By now Kemo became suspicious, but erased it from his thoughts as he argued with himself that one bird could do no harm to his mash. He had changed his sitting position to rest his legs when the bird came back. "I'll be damned!" he said jumping up. "I'm going to see what's going on here." He walked to the top of the ridge and down below, he saw ten thousand drunken blackbirds spreading their wings, but unable to fly.

I Ain't Going

Recently at a Father's day celebration, the Indians at their Community Center, had a charcoaled steak dinner. After much patting of bellies and now and then a "burp," a preacher decided to do a short sermon. He was allowed only a few minutes, but once he started he was frothing at the mouth, waving his hands, stomping the floor—preaching hell's fire and brimstone. It seemed he was pointing out those who had material gain and wealth. People were shaking in their boots, so to speak. He shook a finger saying: "You can't take it with you!" An old and wrinkled Indian in the back row stood up and said defiantly:
"I ain't going!"

The 'Udder Side

In World War I some of the Doughboys (GIs) got leaves to attend a French fair or carnival in Paris. It was one of those supergala festivities, quite relaxing to American soldiers. Two of my cousins (fullblood Indians) were strolling the midway in search of some milk which they had not seen or tasted for so long. Most of the stands were attended by French girls who did not understand or speak English. They (my cousins) stopped at a stand they thought most likely to sell milk, but they too could not speak French nor understand it. One of them asked the girls if they had any milk for sale and added: "Cow's milk—cow's milk—you understand?" The girls chattered with each other—waving their hands and giggling, but came up with "No! no! Comprendez!" The boys then decided to make motions like milking a cow. They would describe a cow's tit as so long and round and began milking it up and down—up and down. All faces brightened up and the girls chattered, laughing and blushing too as they reached under the counter and presented the boys with a tin of condoms.

The Rabbit and the Tarbaby

There was an old lady who owned a small garden and in it she had planted her favorite vegetable – cabbage. This day she was very angry because a rabbit had been entering the garden and eating her plants. She vowed then, "If I ever catch that rabbit I'm going to wring his neck." She thought of how to make a snare or trap to catch him. She remembered having a large chunk of tar and an idea struck her – she would form a tarbaby with it and set it up in the middle of the garden. She reasoned that anything that touched it would be stuck and could not get loose.

That night the rabbit came to fill himself with young and tender cabbage. As he entered the garden he noticed something unusual, like a human being standing in the middle of the cabbage plants. Very bravely he walked up to it, and said: "What are you?" but the thing did not answer him so he punched it in the stomach and said "I'll make you talk," but much as he tried he could not loosen his hand. He punched with the other hand and it stuck. He said: "Oh, so you think I can't kick you," so he did with all of his might, but realizing that he was caught, fear came over him the whole night through.

Came the dawn and the little lady looked towards her garden and saw that her trap had worked. She hurried to the garden and loosened the rabbit from the sticky tar. She took him to her special chicken fattening coop, put him in it and latched the door. She said to him: "There is one thing I'm going to tell you and you will know never to come back here, I'm going to heat some water, scalding hot to pour on you then let you go." With that she went in to her home.

A sly old Fox that had been stealing the old lady's chickens appeared on the scene. Stealthily he peeked around the corner of the chicken house.

He saw the rabbit in the little chicken coop and after seeing all was clear, he crouched low and ran up to it. "Well now my friend, what are you doing in this coop?" he said. The rabbit knew that he had to be very shrewd to outwit the Fox; so he said, "Oh yes my friend, I'm here because I'm to be fed some nice young fryers."

The Fox answered: "Now I know that you do not eat chicken my friend, so I'll let you out and I'll get in and you can latch the door on me." So the transfer was made and the rabbit went his merry way, snickering. He did not go far, but to his favorite hollow stump to see what would happen to the Fox.

The little old lady came out of the house with her iron kettle of scalding hot water and poured it all on the Fox in the coop and then turned him out. He could hardly walk – the pain was excruciating. He would trot a ways then stop to lick himself. He finally came to the stump the rabbit was hidden in. He hopped up on top to rest and cool himself.

The rabbit could hardly wait to search through his bag of cruel tricks. He found a long needle, reached up and punched his friend with it. The fox jumped and cried out: "You old black ants – don't you know I'm in pain!" After scratching his bottom and soothing himself, he quieted down. The rabbit shook all over and could hardly smother his laughing. Once more he reached up and punched his friend again. This time in great fury the Fox shouted and jumped off the stump and simultaneously the rabbit jumped out and ran.

The race was on, the Fox with murder in his eyes tried hopelessly to catch the rabbit who came to his favorite hollow tree and scampered up it, and the fox slid up to the hole. He looked up in the hollow of the tree and shouted:

"So you think that you have outsmarted me, but I'm telling you now that you are sure to die – I'm going to kill you! I will not quit until I do!"

An old owl, a friend of the Fox, flew down and lit on a limb nearby. The fox said to him: "I have a rabbit up this hollow tree and I would like for you to guard this hole and him until I can go borrow an ax to chop it down." "Alright, my friend, I will watch him for you," said the owl. "But I must warn you," said the Fox, "that rabbit is very tricky and you have to watch him very close." "Don't you worry, I'll be here and so will your friend when you get back." So they parted and the fox went to borrow an ax.

The rabbit had been listening and heard everything. He resorted to his bag of tricks again and found a plug of strong chewing tobacco and took a mouthful of it.

"Hey! Mr. Owl look up here. I'm going to give you some expert advice on how to guard a prisoner. You must first look up at me with eyes wide open — I mean real wide." So the owl strained his eyes to see the rabbit and he spat a mouthful of strong tobacco juice into them.

The pain and sting was unbearable to the owl and what's more, he was blind. He ran in wide circles, turning somersaults and the rabbit went his merry way, laughing.

The Fox returned with the ax and saw what had happened and said to the owl: "Didn't I tell you to watch him close — what happened?"

"Oh my friend! It was terrible the fight we had. You see this ground all torn and all those droppings everywhere — well I knocked them out of him, but he got loose and left."

"Well my friend," said the Fox. "I can't blame you for what has happened, but I'm not through with that good-for-nothing rabbit. I'm going to build a fire and gather up all of his droppings and burn them." While he was gathering the wood for the fire, the Owl asked him: "What good would that do?" "Well," the fox answered. "He will die from a lingering illness and maybe instantly." The owl had to think quickly and then he said: "My friend, I must confess that I have told you a lie, all of this fighting I told you didn't happen and those droppings are mine and not the rabbit's."

The Bear Hunt

A Creek Indian hunter grabbed his bow and arrows and high-tailed to bear country, as the season was open to hunt them. A friend in up-state Washington had coached him on how to hunt bears as we don't have them in Oklahoma.

He arrived on the scene of where a giant Grizzly had been seen often in a very rugged area. Cautiously he weaved through a thicket where there were signs of fresh bear tracks. He would stop and listen. . . slithering through tall grass. Once or twice he stopped to let his heart calm down. Suddenly, from behind, a giant black grizzly grabbed him around his chest, a typical bear hug so hard that he could hardly breathe. He had to think quickly as to what to do to try and free himself. Luckily, he had one free hand, so he began to rub the bear's belly. He gradually lowered his rubbing and as he did the monster slackened his hold a bit. He began to fondle his privates which caused the bear to free him and fall backwards flat on his back. The hunter ran as fast as he could until he was nearly fifty yards away. Stopping, he looked to see why the bear didn't chase him. To his surprise he saw it laying flat on its back and motioning him with those giant paws and claws to come back – come back.

Clan Worship

My bro-in-law, Sleeping Panther;
    was strong bear clan.
He's gone now to high country
    – beyond the north star.
He drank Coors, no other brew
    – he said it best.
I ask why he drank Coors?
    he said it best!
He said it come from bear country
    where pure clean waters are.
I say, others come from pure clean
        waters too.
He say I like Coors best
    because bear wade and piss
    in those clear mountain streams
    – make good medicine.

71

Phase III

(Catharsis)

Big white waterbird (Wa'dola)
Sailed in to land on gravel bar
    —failed to judge speed
        took three steps
        —imperfect landing.
    (My words)
Next time he lands, but
      bounce up and down
      almost perfect.
    (My words)
Must be silent as shadow—
      fold wings, coordinate
      with soft step down
  So crayfish, minnows and helgramites
      do not know presence.
      Perfect.
    (My Words)
But who is Wadola that he
    should splash my words
    with white digested crayfish
    —white acculturation!

Non Decorum

My old grandpa (Chápōcha)
   wrinkled and old
Sits in deep thought.
Hightop boots – black hat
banded with red and blue
      beads
eagle feathers black tipped
on left side – straight up.
Leaning on seedick kega
chin resting on gnarled hands
      overlapping;
mouth pooched like
   end of mushroom
I do mental telepathy
   read his thoughts:
like in Kaleidoscope
   Some hold long
   some change
      deranged.

Deer walking in snow –
   wary – sniffing air
Arrow nocked – tension,
Bow drawn – 60 pounds –

He follows her to
   the rendezvous
   big woman, rear
      like Hippo.
Mushroom mouth spreads
   slightly – smiles;
She stoops – whips dress
   over back –

Prepare your self
  old man!
I came to kill you.
  quick knives flash
  in sun light.

Like Cougar — Low-Low —
      Spring set
      tail twitching
Split-second grappling —

Ninety years now
  he feels his side
  sharp rheumatic pains
from old wound —

Visits old grave of friend
  few mussel shells there
  — hmm.

My old woman
  skins and dresses
      deer
I eat raw melt — warm —

Slowly I approach
  Hippo woman,
holding penis
  like ear corn —
The bird! — The bird!
    it carries messages!
      iyee-hanh —
        She sighed.

seedick kega: walking stick

74

Hoot Owls Roast an Indian

I was camped on the Baron Fork crick when the following conversation of owls took place. Interpretations are in parentheses.

Who who – whowho – ah!
(I've found an Indian in a whiteman's tent.)
Who Who – who who,
who who – who' who whooooo Ah?
(shall I call the others?)
Who.
(Yes) Four or five gather together in a tree overhead.
Who who – who who Ah
(Look – he has a Coleman lantern and stove!)
(They laugh.)
Ah Ah Ah – who ah!
(. . . and look at those rods and reels!)
Who – Oooooo!
(A Coleman ice chest)
Whooooe!
(Do you see what I see?)
Who?
(A pair of women's stockings on the back of a chaise
lounge chair!)
Whoooo!
(I'll bet a fat mouse he hasn't caught a fish, and
don't expect to!!)
They all laugh.
Who who Ahaaa! Ah Ah Ah!
Who Ah – Ah Ah Ah.

PART FOUR:

Center of the Spirit

The Deerhorn Sweat

There are rituals, ceremonies and religions practised by every race and tribe of mankind. As far back as the Stone Age there are indications and evidences of this fact. Man struggled to try and understand the "unknown." He felt forsaken, but searched for some sign or token – some guideline that would free him of the destitution he was experiencing. Being animal yet having intelligence beyond the reasoning of an animal, he exercised the power to think of things mystifying.

So the Indian – the American Indian, of the redclay mold of Adam, lived in an Eden of pristine surroundings, new born with a pure and undefiled mind. The good spirits revealed to him through dreams and visions, the way of life for his kind. Laid before him were the laws most suitable for his social behaviors, survival and well being. Therefore, he instituted a special ritual and ceremony for a sweatbath.

True, there were many streams and rivers that he bathed in for refreshing and cleansing the body, but it was insufficient for the lack of a ceremony to strengthen his spiritual build through meditation and prayer to draw himself closer to the Great Spirit.

So in the case of my people the Muskogee or Creek tribe, the ritual of the "Sauna" varied in practice. Where an individual desired a simple "sweat" he used a tea made from an herb the "Mintha Longifilia," or the large species of Horsemint. He poured the tea over hot rocks in his type of lodge. Other tribes used roots and herbs such as Cedar, sweetgrass and white sage as we do also for various purposes.

I will now describe a sweat that I participated in a few years ago. The setting was ideal with the tall Beech, Spruce and Birch trees and a typical trout stream winding through it, swift and cold as it was in the month of April. There were indications that other sweats had been held here.

In this event there were four Oklahoma Indian tribes represented, namely: Cheyenne, Muskogee (Creek), Shawnee and Cherokee. Our host was of the Abenaki and Metis.

While we were back in Mecosta, Michigan, we had picked and sorted out twenty-five lava rocks from off the farm of our brother Carroll Arnett and hauled them to this particular Sweat lodge. This species of rock was preferred over others since it would hold heat longer.

The ritual and ceremony of the Indian's sweat bath is somewhat similar to the Swedish sauna and the Turkish sweat, as I have mentioned, but much more interrelated to the spiritual and esoteric.

To make our event more complete we had with us a Priest of the old Native American church from the Cheyenne tribe. He was the master of ceremonies as it should be. Under his direction we arose with the sun to prepare the lodge, which entailed the gathering of wood, the placing of the rocks, etc. The getting of wood was no problem and we had enough to generate heat for at least four hours.

In the mean time the lodge, a dome shaped structure, is built of green poles, whose center height is about fire feet and is large enough to house at least six people. The roof covering is of any material that would hold in the heat of steam. A hole was dug out in the floor of the hut deep enough to hold at least seven sizable rocks.

In addition to the building of the lodge, the fire and a protective lean-to, which we used as a dressing room, one more important structure was completed. Directly in front of the lodge entrance, about a pace away, two forked sticks about a foot long, were stuck in the ground, fourteen inches apart. A cross-bar was laid across and underneath was placed the left deer horn and by it a rope of sweetgrass.

From dawn until around two o'clock in the afternoon we had not taken in any food or drink as it was taboo. We stripped and used towels for loin cloths and welcomed the warmth of the fire as the temperature was 39° and cloudy. Each took his turn to tend the fire.

The purpose of this particular type of sweat was not only to induce perspiration which eliminates poisons in the blood and cleanses the skin, but to rededicate our lives to the Great Spirit.

Nearing the time the ritual and ceremony is to take place, not much is said. If there was any conversation it was in low tones and subdued. As for my thoughts, as I studied the changed color of those black lava rocks, which now from intense heat, had turned to a rose madder hue, I wondered about the Indians who had lived here for ages. I visualized the home of the Iroquois – their lodges along this clear and enchanting stream. The hunter with his longbow, wife and children, wearily returning from the many springs of Saratoga. I wondered about the Adirondack mountains, its flora and fauna – its wild life, whether it was free of pollution. I thought of how the Great Spirit had given us the knowledge to purify ourselves both physically and mentally, and we are here to give thanks for the perpetuation of our well being.

Nothing but an occasional sputter and a tiny pop! among the coals of fire and the gurgle of the brook swirling around little boulders was heard. The Priest, with a "switch" of sage touched it to the fire, came to each one of us in the circle and began to "smoke" us – first to the bottoms of our feet, under our outstretched arms, up and down our sides and the sides of our face. Hot rocks were placed in the pit provided in the lodge.

I being the elder was seated at the right of the door on the inside. Others took their place as directed by the Priest, and he was the last to enter with a bucket of water, the deer horn and sweetgrass. The deer horn was raked over the red hot rocks as if to arrange them to a certain position. The person not participating covered the door opening, pressed down the edges of the hut to make it air tight as possible. We were in darkness and for a few minutes, we each prayed either audibly or silently.

The first water was poured slowly over the rocks and a soft "sigh" was emitted. A small box of cedar needles and a sheaf of sweetgrass or sage was passed around and we knew what to do with it. The first heat of steam was barely warm, but the scent of sage and burnt deer horn permeated the air in the hut.

The pouring of water was done at intervals of six to eight minutes. Each time the heat of steam intensified and one felt suffocation. After the fourth pouring it was like being under a shower with the hottest water possible from the hot water tank. I felt miserable. In about forty-five minutes the Priest ordered the door to be opened. We filed out scraping the sweat from our face, arms and legs.

In a little while our body temperature became oriented to the outside, but we had one more thing to do and that was to rush to the cold running water of the stream and wash ourselves off. It took a lot of grit and stamina to do this – and *invigorating* was a mild word for it. We dried ourselves and once in our clothes, we felt so clean and as light as a feather and as hungry as a wolf.

June 2, '82

The Mound

A mold has sprouted on the Mound
   a far cry from Tokepatcha town.
A thing delectable, yet powerful,
The Tase Kia home of the Muskogee people.
The Chief seated with his Abok-ta
   and precious person Hemeha,
   surrounded by the seven clans,
   and the Tusknuggies.
Thus the Creek Court of Law.
The ball clubs and Buffalo skull
of the ancient pole is no more.
I am of that ancient blood
I speak its tongue fluently.
I have been scratched and named
Partook of that king of medicines
   Meko hoyv mecha.
I have sweated over stones
   with mint and sage
I know of the sacred fire
   around which we danced
      to day break.
         Wotko. . . Okisce!

Songs on Winding Trails

June 14, 1987

Straight paths made by man
are unnatural and full of curses,
But a trail is a song
That animals sing as they go.
The oldest trail is to the spring.
Mountain sheep and goats' trails
around the boulders, crags and cliffs
Only scent is their marker
In their citadel of peace.

So Small

October 5, 1988

The swift running creek, the gurgling brook
      preach a better sermon
Than any mortal could ever do.
I turn the pages of its scripture
To better understand Creation.
In this quietness and solitude,
A tall, white-bearded mountain points
To infinity – the great beyond!
I feel much smaller than the mites
In these cool and shaded waters.

Eulogy on a Great Creek Poet

If I may, and the gods be willing, use the poet's license and borrow a phrase from William Shakespeare's Anthony, and I quote: "I come not to bury Caesar, but to praise him." So I say to you, by beloved people of the Creek Indian nation, who are inclined and gifted in the literary arts and to those of my white brother writers, consider my praise for the greatest Creek Indian poet known. Yes – he is gone from us – gone to his glory – yet a part of him lives to this day – the book of poems that he wrote – and I'm speaking of Alexander L. Posey.

He was to the ancient Creeks what Hiawatha was to the Iroquois and what Manabozho was to the Algonquins. . . a great leader, an intellectual. Born Indian of a feared Clan of the Wind in line of the Harjos. But most of all he was a true lover of nature.

As he walked his Taledega, his favorite wooded area, the flowers bowed in obesance, hawks and eagles swooped down to greet him, the meadow lark sang its best aria and the deer were not afraid of him. He understood the language of the babbling brook, the bees brought ambrosia to his lips and his pen recorded the joys of them. Oh my soul – I would that I could walk in his moccasins – just for one day.

He felt in his soul there was more he could do in his life. His energy and exuberance for what holds forth boosted him on to higher goals. He so desired public officialdom that in a short while he attained it. He became well known for his administrative ability. Did valuable service for the Creek tribe in organizing schools and orphanages. He related ancient Creek folklore and recalled the names of wise old men now forgotten.

He had built enough merit for himself as a public official and a proven administrator that it seemed he was bound for higher stakes in the affairs of his people and the United States Government. But sad to say – it was not to be. Nature and his beloved Taledega was calling him back – his pen urging him to extol more of his very being – he felt it in his very nerve fiber that he was being drawn by an unknown force to go back home to the earthly ones, the Common Things.

Was it premonition or an ill boding, that he wrote in his book of poems the following:

Why do trees along the river
  Lean so far out o'er the tide?
Very wise men tell me why, but
  I am never satisfied;
And so I keep my fancy still,
  That trees lean out to save
the drowning from the clutches of
the cold remorseless wave.

Was it he was torn from an ambition to climb the ladder higher to fame and fortune which was within his grasp? Was it his people were prejudiced and showed a tendency to disown him?

It is history now that he attempted to cross a wild and rampaging river – his own river by his Taledega.

One slip of his foot and the swift current carried him down stream. He grasped at the very trees he spoke of that tried to save him. Hanging on to a frail willow limb, his last hope, but his grasp gave way and the river swallowed him into eternity.

Why-oh why-was fate so remorseless, why such a tragedy to a man who might have been the hopes of his tribe or to his country? The heartbreak of it all is to know he was only a score and seventeen years young.

I did not know Alexander Posey personally, but we were of the same genre – of "one fire" according to Creek tribal family relationship. Had he lived or even now, I feel that the laurels of a poet should have been conferred upon him.

I shall burn cedar often to his memory and may there be mussel shells over his grave. I quote here one of his many poems which could serve as his epitaph.

When death has shut the blue sky out from me
        Sweet daffodil,
And years roll on without my memory,
Thou'lt reach thy tender fingers down to mine of clay,
        a true friend still.
Altho I'll never know thee till the judgement day.

Wotko Okisce!

Salute to Alexander Posey

As you walked your Taledega*
The beauty of nature was on your mind,
You held back the welling tears.
Ahead of you Tos'kë chatters*
Heralding your appearance.
All of nature bows to you
I too bend my knees.
I feel we were of one genre.
You preferred Chennube Harjo
To be a name of your choice
Your old ones were of that clan.
It may seem ridiculous
For an Indian of political stance
To give praise to a Daffodil,
But deep down you were a poet
Most worthy of a crown of Laurel,
Worthy of the Creek people –
Worthy of having an Em pona'ya*
      Wōtkō okisce!*

*Taledega – Foothills of a mountain range on the Canadian River
*Tos'kë – Speckled sapsucker that warns someone is coming
*Em pona'ya – One who speaks for another
*Wōtkō okisce! – I of the Racoon clan, have spoken.

Impromptu

Walking barefoot on long
      sand bar soft and white
south wind twirling my eagle feather
−find long stick−I write,
      walking backwards,
much wisdom the world should know
−much hurry−sand eats wood fast
for I'll forget, when wood is gone,
      Just what I wrote.
There'll be other sand bars forming
      −other sticks adrift,
but I will be too old then
      to remember.

Wahelá Pana (Ant Lion)

Why write of Wahelá pana?
    It is in a song as old as time.
I cannot sing it—I dare not.
    It is buried in a pyramid
        upside down;
    built to exacting mathematical proficiency
—a cone of cascading fine dust
    and it, at the bottom—hidden.
        (It is in a song)
One foolish thought and its calculated risk
        would crumble—
    creation would be a farce.
Each finitesmal grain of dust holds
        the wall intact.
One single thought of Survival
Would start an avalanche of
        Nothingness.
The unwary, the reckless
—those of one track minds
Fall into Wahelá pana's trap.
        (It is in a Song.)

No Caviar

I'm not the leaden-eyed spider,
Adorned with a white mustache,
But one mathematical with
Knowledge and understanding
Of elipses and hyperboles.
Building webs to perfection
To snare ponderosities
Of the rich and snobbish elite –
I train my webs not to hold
Their esoteric cogitations,
Superficial sentimentalities,
Platitudinous ponderosities,
But to savor simplicity,
Like the language of the hill-billies
Life sustaining cornbread and beans –
And a jug of panther sweat.

My Haunt

Yes, Yes, my wild and yellow rose,
I knew you when you pushed up clods
And now you brush my feathers
By this crooked and gravely path,
That winds down to Sycamore springs.
I see you my young beloved,
Whose balm is heady as yours.
Would that she were winding down with me.
Spirits of yore made this path
That's bedecked with Huckleberries sweet —
Hanging purple Haws and plums —
            and there, the spring of cold, cold water,
filling a translucent rocky puddle
where oft a Diamond Rattler lays —
            away from summer's sweltering heat.

Indian Flute

I hear sweet sound of it.
To my mind – it is Aeolian
– a narcosis, lulling all of me.
I sit by stream against big rock
       – by singing little waters
       by white bearded mountains.
See Eagle flying lazy,
See fish with rainbow colors
       Tall Spruce – Quaker aspens.
My Spirit rises and falls
like breath – I dream.
Blow – blow – blow
  Oh charming flute.
I close my heavy eyes;
Your music brings to me
       Caresses of my love.
Bring her not to me –
  No! no! no! not now
– or I will die, seeing – feeling
reality.

Seeing, but not Believing

August 21, 1987

'Twas by the Brook of Cedars
That Wotko played his flute,
Off to himself by trickling waters
To while away his longing thoughts
of E-nah-gayah, the Creek Princess.
On a warpath he saw her once
In a dream, that seemed so real
that she came and touched his lips;
A fire was lit in his heart.
While on a tune he was playing
He wondered then if she was real.
The lulling tune became hypnotic
So that he fell into slumber.
The princess came singing softly
The Indian Love Call of ages past.
Awakened, he saw the form by him,
and asked, "Este to yec kv?"*

Are you human?

97

An Ant's Highway

A thought struck me as I wandered about,
And saw an Ant's highway – a caravan,
Through a dense forest of entanglements.
I squatted to study this industrial event.
Came to mind our system of highways
The law of commercial distribution of goods.
Would that I could visit the Ant's kingdom
Way down, not high as our skyscrapers.
I'd find no mechanism, no computers,
No electrical musts, or giant cabinets,
Filled with drawers of business information.
But feel that intuition guides them –
A spirit of nature since the beginning of time.
Could not the Indian survive as the Ant?

Poetry Dead?

I heard them saying, while in my den,
That poetry is dead and buried alive.
So, I lick my paws and belly
    and prepare to hibernate.
I'm tired of technical innovators
The forked tongue of Anglo Saxon linguists
Articulating like rocks down a chute.
Is that fluent and poetic rhythm?
I don't write for the intelligentsia
Native Americans pen cliches
And try to put the scent of roses
The flight of the Eagle – the gurgling brook
All that's beautiful on to paper.
"Poetry is efficacious."

Center of the Spirit

The Center of the Spirit is like a hub
   whose spokes are paths of moccasin tracks
   made by our ancient ones.
Here was once their Eden, their paradise
   as far as the eye could see
   and beyond from sea to sea
   and back to the center of the spirit
      the circle – unbroken.
If we could resurrect those bones
     of our native ancestors,
     and if we could see this land
     still in its primitive state
Unpolluted . . . free of toxic wastes –
   then it was truly a haven,
      For the redman.
But I, an Indian, look about and wonder
     why the whiteman calls it progress
   to lay waste the land – pollute the air
     poison our minds with all gold that glitters!

There may be no amber waves of grain
. . . no purple mountain tops
When progress has reached its limitations
And all that's left is a smoking heap
     of scattered bones and rubble.

January, '86

Creek Thought No. 9

I speak a language older than English
I walk the land of my origin.
It has been said and is of truth
There's nothing new under the sun.
We with feathers and drums stand by
Watching whiteman disbelieving
How we managed to survive.
He overly educates himself
In science and technology —
Is blind to its consequences.
Does not know he has a choice
To live or destroy himself.

Turn Back! Whiteman

Neither pagan nor heathen were my people,
Free of idolatry in the fullest sense,
but aware of one who created them.
The hordes of whites who assaulted our shores
Were pious frauds – paganistic.
In the days of my old ones
Alcohol was not known
Or narcotics of any sort.
They knew not of the devil
Nor the fiery pits of Hell,
In fact, we have no word for them;
Yet the whiteman says the Indians
Should be cleansed of dark sins;
So hypocritical they have been.
They should take stock of themselves.
They want we, the native Americans,
To don a business suit – get in the swim,
So that we can go to Hell together.
How can the white race be told the truth
Of the doom they are creating?
Back up – back up! my white brother,
Your starwars and trillions of dollars
Make you blind to your madness.
Why do you commit yourself
To jump the cliff to your death?
Wake up! Wake up! Turn back! Turn back!

102

Phase I

Here I am – eighty moons
    of garbage
I have not completed the hoop.
  It has a gap, rolls limping
    and wobbly
      falls flat;
Not graceful like a silver dollar
    that spins and wavers
      in a circle
      faster-faster-faster
    then falls with silvery ease.
Like a hunter jumping a rabbit,
    in the snow,
  that has a trick of running
    in a wide circle.
The hunter tracks with confidence,
the rabbit retraces its foot prints
    in the circle
jumps out to the side, cutting the circle,
    buries itself in the snow.
The hunter steadily tracks
  erasing all foot prints
    circling – circling – circling.

Phase II

I, Indian hear someone say:
  "time flies and waits for no man."
I ate it up in my youth
    – turn clock back;
And now time owes me.
In my eighty years I'm
    in lock-step with time,
      it ticks
      I tock.

Seven Hawks

Impromptu, for my friend, Joe

September – cornfields of stubs and blades,
Air humid, stiffling, dust devils form
In tiny swirls, growing, towering
Reaching a hawk high in the sky.
She clucks and Screams – KEEeees!!
Does Aerobatics – then out of sight.

I know these hawks that grew nearby
Two hens, three males, nature's oddity.
Up that tall hickory tree
A shoddy nest of twigs and leaves
Fell quails fat onto my plate
The mother meant well, but the chicks
Nudged their morsel overboard.

To initiate the young ones
The Seven hawks wind into the blue
Circling, circling, higher and higher
Until the breath of many wings
Gives birth to dust devils
That mystify the minds of men.

The whirlwinds gone and are no more
And now there are Seven hawks
Leaving, leaving me once more
High, high in yonder blue
Circling, circling – klucking, KEEeees!
Joining a trade wind – gone for the winter.